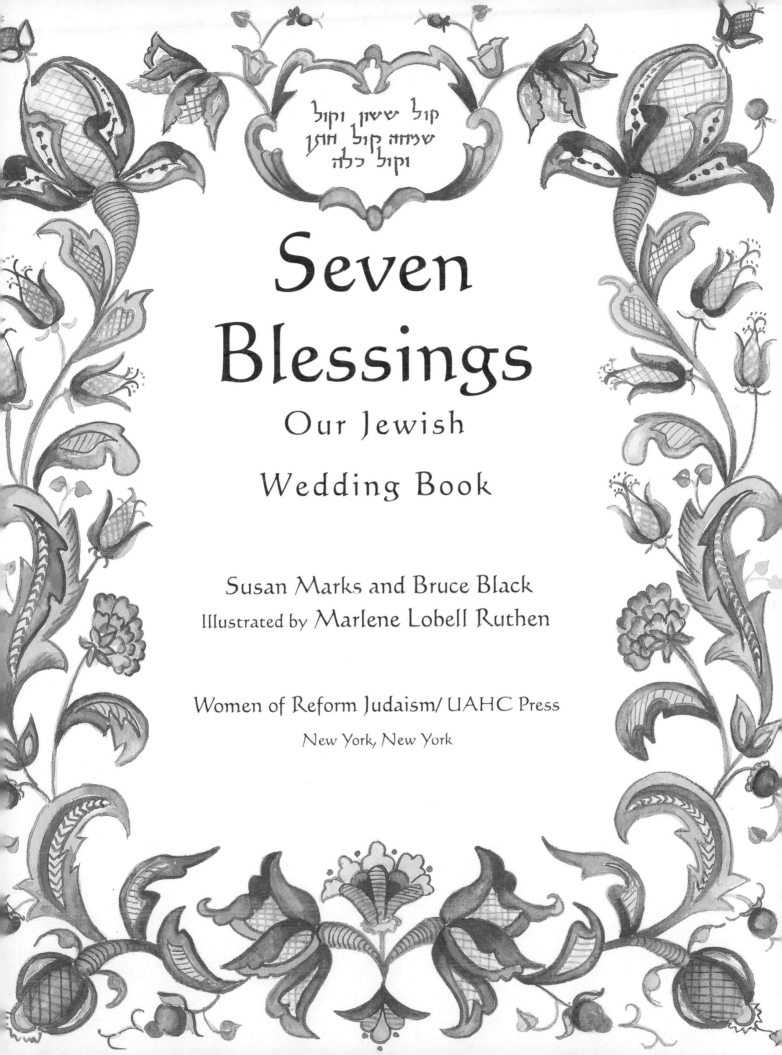

קול ששון וקול
שמחה קול חתן
וקול כלה

Seven Blessings

Our Jewish

Wedding Book

Susan Marks and Bruce Black

Illustrated by Marlene Lobell Ruthen

Women of Reform Judaism/ UAHC Press

New York, New York

The *Sheva Berachot* are reprinted from the *Rabbi's Manual* © 1988 by the Central
Conference of American Rabbis. With permission.

This book is printed on acid-free paper.
Manufactured in the United States of America

10   9   8   7   6   5   4   3   2   1

"A marriage partner is from the Holy One....At times, a man is led to his wife; at other times, a woman is led to her husband."
Genesis Rabbah 68:3

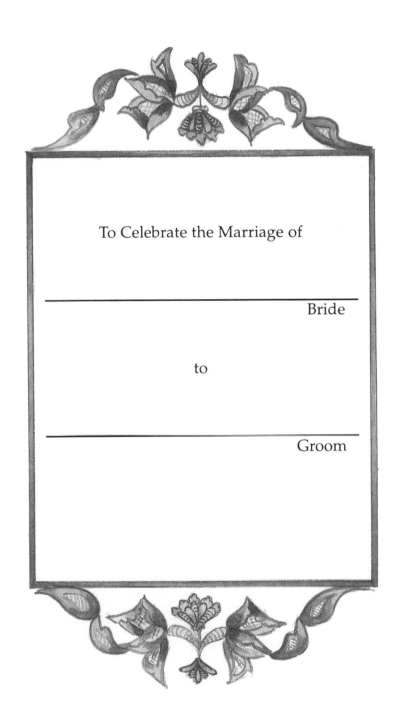

To Celebrate the Marriage of

_____

Bride

to

_____

Groom

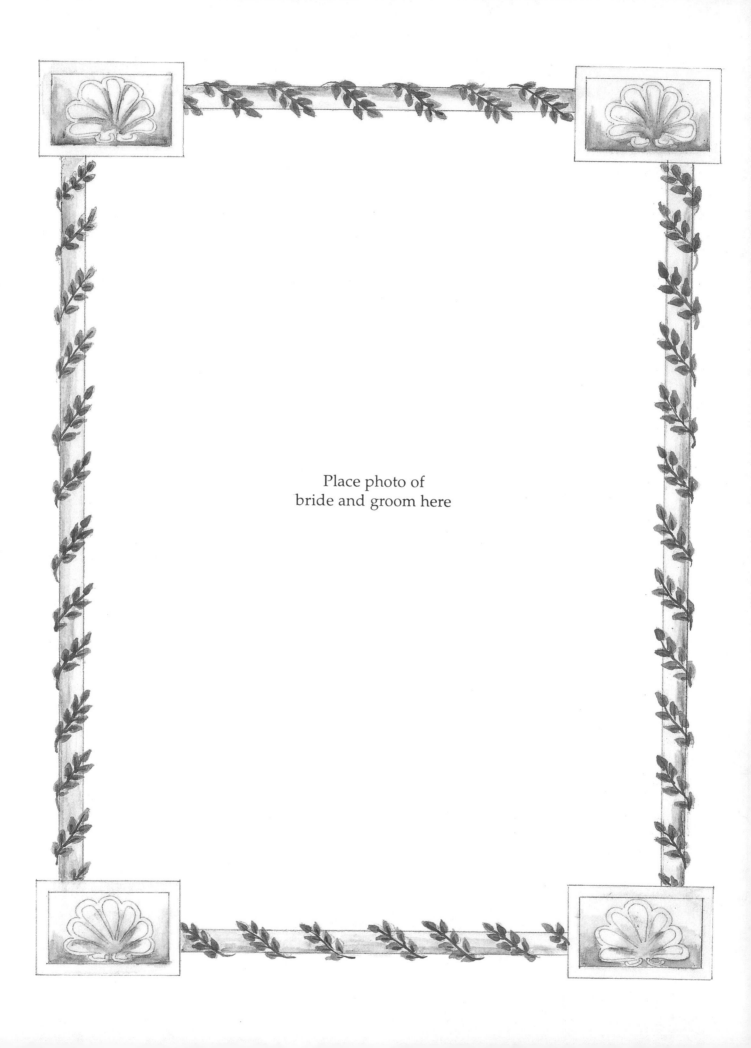

Place photo of
bride and groom here

בסימן טוב

Contents

Introduction

Mazal Tov! Congratulations! Chances are that you are opening this book because you have recently become engaged. We hope this book, *Seven Blessings*, gives both of you the opportunity to explore together the many preparations that will present themselves as your wedding day approaches.

We chose this title for two reasons. First, it echoes the Seven Blessings or *Sheva Berachot* recited at the conclusion of the marriage service. These blessings accompany the concluding glass of wine under the *chupah* and explore the cosmic connection between husband and wife. Second, we believe that marriage—and preparation for marriage—offers each individual myriad opportunities that are indeed blessings. From the smallest decision to the largest choice, the process of becoming husband and wife leads to many challenging situations and hopeful possibilities. As you begin your journey together, we hope this book gives you a chance to articulate your concerns, laugh at the difficulties, and, yes, even count your blessings.

Ultimately a wedding, any wedding, is about creating a home. This is especially true of a Jewish marriage, where the home is the center of so much of our people's traditions. No wonder the home stands symbolically in the center of the wedding itself in the guise of a *chupah*. For this reason you will find the section of this book that explores the creation of your home in the middle rather than at the end after the wedding, as is the case with so many wedding books. If any section is left incomplete as you create this interactive record together, let it not be the one devoted to establishing your home.

You will no doubt have questions and concerns that are not addressed in these pages. This book is not designed to take the place of your meetings with the rabbi or even your own research into some of the particulars of

Jewish wedding traditions.* Rather, this book is meant to serve as a log for recording your explorations of all these traditions, ancient and modern. No other wedding will be identical to yours; yet by this celebration you take your place with generations of brides and grooms.

Three symbols describe the core of the Jewish wedding. The first is the *chupah*, which symbolizes the home. Whatever form the *chupah* takes in your service–whether a simple *tallit* or an elaborate floral canopy–you are symbolically entering your own shared threshold, marking your move from the public "single" world to the private world of a "couple" and stepping into the home in which you will consummate your marriage.

The *ketubah* is a profound symbol, too. At the root of a *ketubah*–no matter its language, the simplicity or complexity of its design, or the people chosen as witnesses–is a covenant between bride and groom. This covenant mirrors the convenantal commitment shared by God and the people Israel at Mount Sinai. In talmudic times the groom guaranteed certain monies to support his wife if, heaven forbid, there was a divorce or he died. But the *ketubah's* message of commitment has come to include much more. Many couples today use the *ketubah* to establish an egalitarian framework for their marital commitments.

Finally, a formal transaction must take place. In other eras this was signified by the giving of a coin. Over time the coin was replaced by a ring of equal value, which has in its very design the beauty of symbolizing eternity.

These three symbols–*chupah, ketubah,* and ring–grew from the legal core of what constitutes a Jewish marriage. The rest is commentary! For instance, the *Sheva Berachot* or Seven Blessings recited at the conclusion of the marriage service are a poetic vision that links your wedding with the creation of man and woman, as well as the Creation itself.

*There are wonderful resources available, and we hope you enjoy your further study. Especially informative, conveying a broad spectrum of choices and practices, is Anita Diamant's *The New Jewish Wedding*. Rabbi Daniel B. Syme's *The Jewish Wedding Book* carefully explains traditions and shares beautiful illustrations from many eras. Both books are available in many Jewish libraries.

Seven nights of dinners, which immediately follow the wedding, also take the name Seven Blessings, *Sheva Berachot*. At these dinners, friends entertain the groom and bride, helping them to make the transition to married life. After all, until recently a bride and groom may not have met each other until their wedding day. In modern times, for some Jews, a honeymoon may replace these seven dinners, but the celebratory language of these blessings carries the bride and groom forward into their marriage.

Sheva Berachot

We praise You, *Adonai* our God, Ruler of the universe, Creator of the fruit of the vine.

We praise You, *Adonai* our God, Ruler of the universe, Creator of all things for Your glory.

We praise You, *Adonai* our God, Ruler of the universe, Creator of man and woman.

We praise You, *Adonai* our God, Ruler of the universe, who creates us to share with You in life's everlasting renewal.

We praise You, *Adonai* our God, who causes Zion to rejoice in her children's happy return.

We praise You, *Adonai* our God, who causes bride and groom to rejoice. May these loving companions rejoice as have Your creatures since the days of Creation.

We praise You, *Adonai* our God, Ruler of the universe, Creator of joy and gladness, bride and groom, love and kinship, peace and friendship. O God, may there always be heard in the cities of Israel and in the streets of Jerusalem: the sounds of joy and of happiness, the voice of the groom and the voice of the bride, the shouts of young people celebrating, and the songs of children at play. We praise You, *Adonai* our God, who causes the bride and groom to rejoice together.

May the months and years ahead be filled with great creativity and great blessings for you and all those you love. Again, *Mazal Tov!*

January 1997　　　　　　　　　　　　　　　　　　*Rabbi Susan Marks*
Tevet 5757　　　　　　　　　　　　　　　　　　　　　*Bruce Black*

Place early courtship
photo here

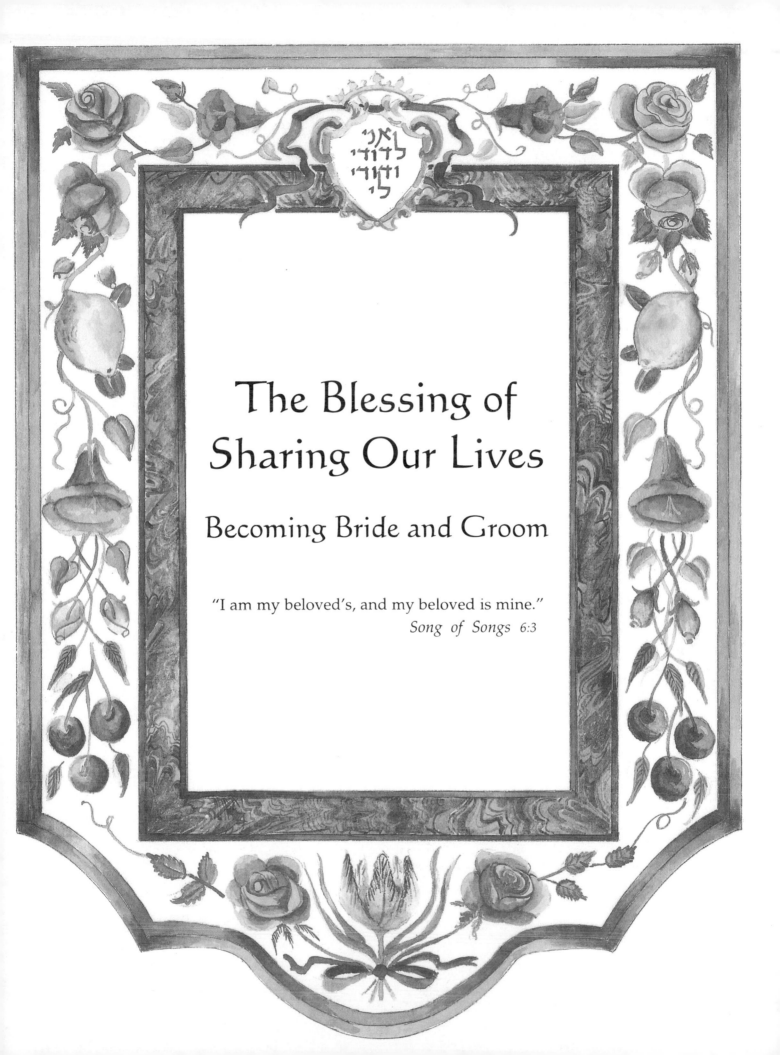

אֲנִי לְדוֹדִי וְדוֹדִי לִי

The Blessing of Sharing Our Lives

Becoming Bride and Groom

"I am my beloved's, and my beloved is mine."
Song of Songs 6:3

What We See When

Bride

What first attracted you to him?

How does he differ *most* from you?

How are you *exactly* like him?

We Look At Each Other

Groom

What first attracted you to her?

How does she differ *most* from you?

How are you *exactly* like her?

Our Separate Histories

Bride's Family and History

Family members

Learning to see my family through his eyes

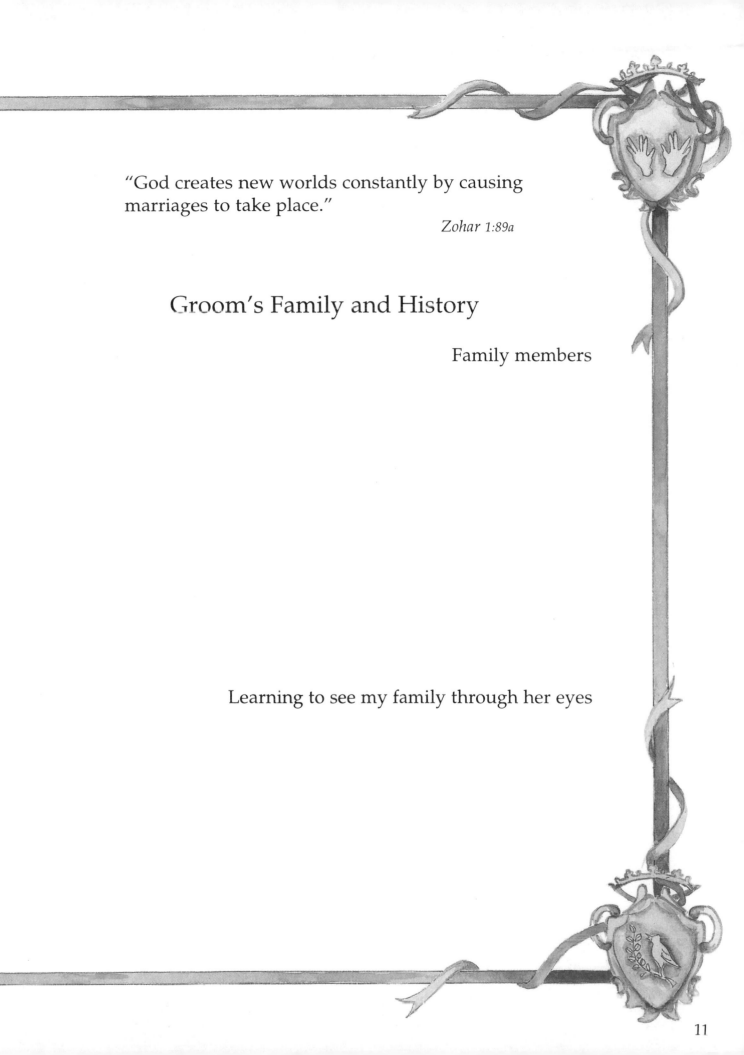

"God creates new worlds constantly by causing marriages to take place."

Zohar 1:89a

Groom's Family and History

Family members

Learning to see my family through her eyes

Our Courtship

How we met

"Give me the kisses of your mouth. For your love is more delightful than wine."

Song of Songs 1:2

Our first dates

Making the Commitment:

God brought Adam and Eve together, saying,

How we became engaged

When our engagement occurred

Our Engagement

"It is not good to be alone." –*from Genesis 2:18*

Where it took place

Additional impressions

Place engagement
photo here

The Blessing of Community

Inviting Friends and Family

"May there always be heard in the cities of Israel and in the streets of Jerusalem...the voice of the groom and the voice of the bride and the shouts of young people celebrating."

from the Sheva Berachot

Sharing the News

How we told people

Reactions

Announcements

Prewedding Celebrations

Place special prewedding
celebration photo here

Over time Jews have developed different customs to prepare for marriage, such as bridal showers, bachelor dinners, engagement parties, an *aufruf*, rehearsal dinners, and visiting a *mikveh*. You probably will observe some of these and perhaps others.

Anecdotes

Invitation

Place invitation here

"Among those obligations whose reward is without measure is rejoicing with the bride and groom."
from the Morning Prayer Service

Guest List

Name and Address	Number Invited	Number Accepted

Guest List

Name and Address	Number Invited	Number Accepted

Name and Address

Number
Invited

Number
Accepted

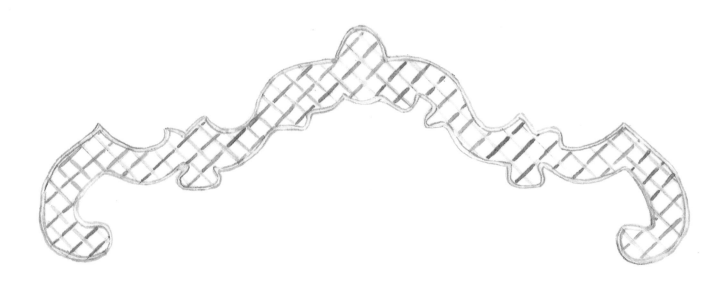

Place photo of bride and
groom preparing
their home here

עד שמצאתי את שאהבה נפשי

The Blessing of a Home Together

Preparing Our Home

"Write them on the doorposts of your house and on your gates."

Deuteronomy 6:9

Registering for Gifts

Our Table

Daily Use

China pattern

Flatware

Glassware

Other gifts

Festival Settings

China pattern

Flatware

Glassware

Other gifts

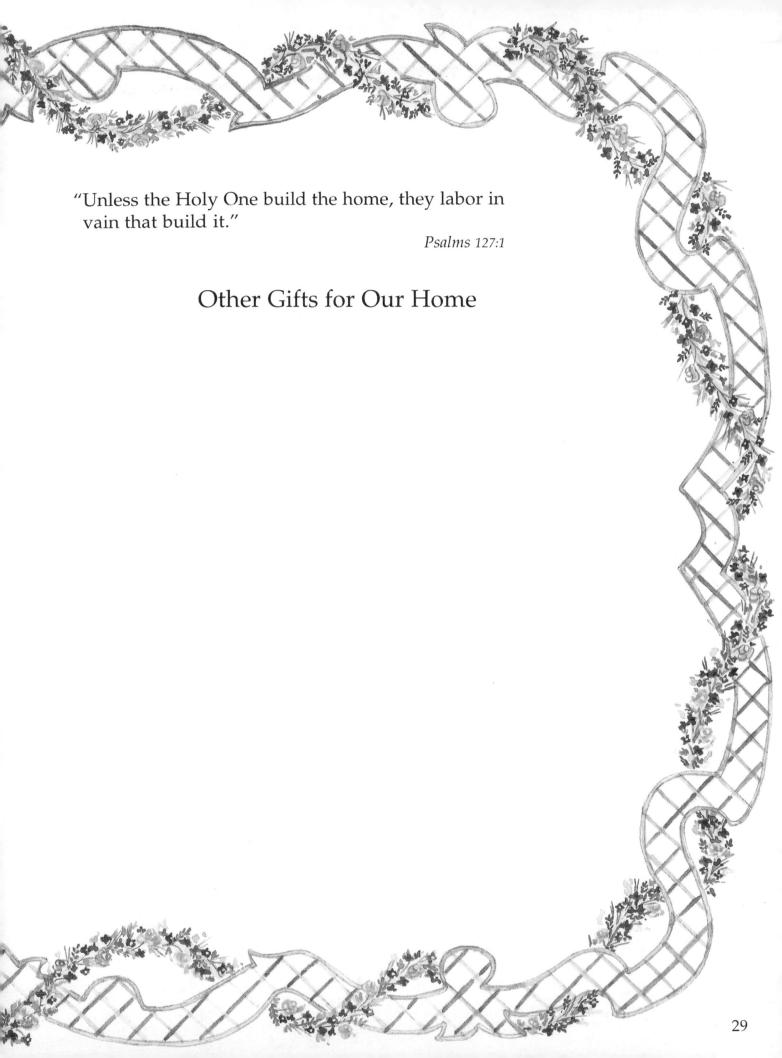

"Unless the Holy One build the home, they labor in vain that build it."

Psalms 127:1

Other Gifts for Our Home

Ritual Objects for the Home

Mezuzah

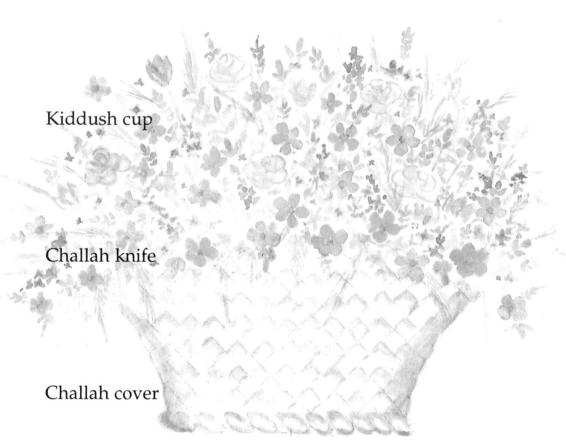

Kiddush cup

Challah knife

Challah cover

"Where a husband and wife are worthy, the Shechinah dwells with them."

Babylonian Talmud Sotah   17a

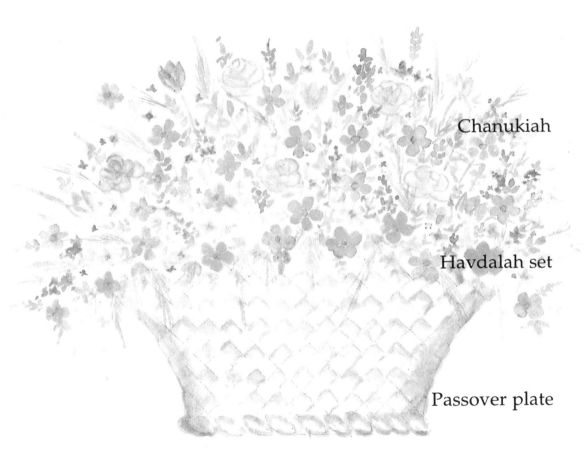

Candleholders

Chanukiah

Havdalah set

Passover plate

Intangible Building Blocks:

A *ketubah* hanging prominently in a couple's home
partner. To this day it speaks of a husband and wife

By What Qualities Do We

Emotional qualities

Intellectual qualities

Creating a Special Place

traditionally spoke of security for the less protected
caring for each other.

Want Our Home Enriched?

Spiritual qualities

Cultural qualities

Place photo of bride and
groom preparing for the
wedding with friends or
family here

בסימנא
טבא

ואֲרַשְׂתִּיךְ לִי לְעוֹלָם

The Blessing of
Tradition

Arranging for the
Wedding

"I shall betroth you to me forever."
Hosea 2:21

Preparing for the Ceremony

Picking out rings

Selecting a rabbi or cantor

Choosing or writing a ketubah

Finding or constructing the chupah

Deciding on witnesses

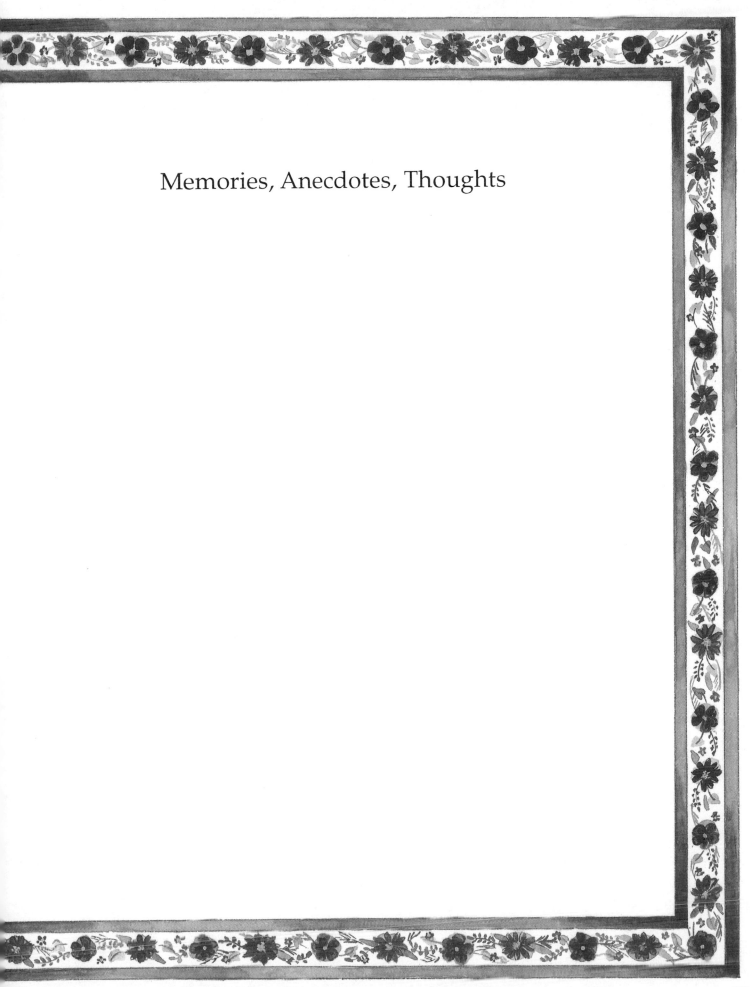

Memories, Anecdotes, Thoughts

Preparing for the Wedding Party

In keeping with the principle of *Hiddur Mitzvah*, "the adornment of a commandment,"we celebrate God by making beautiful the things used in the observance of a *mitzvah*.

Bride's dress/wedding gown

Attendants' dresses

Flowers

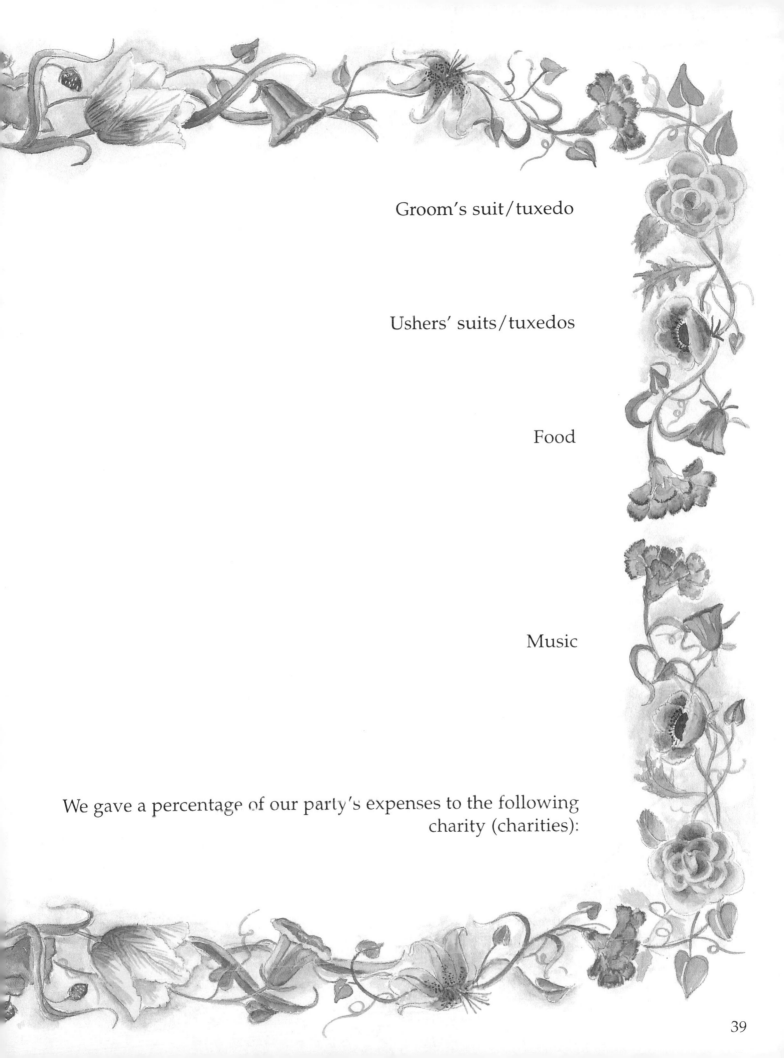

Groom's suit/tuxedo

Ushers' suits/tuxedos

Food

Music

We gave a percentage of our party's expenses to the following charity (charities):

Place humorous
prewedding photo here

The Blessing of Laughter

Keeping a Sense of Humor

"Once a Roman woman asked a rabbi, 'In how many days did God create the world?' The rabbi replied, 'In six.' She asked, 'What has God been doing since?' The rabbi replied: 'God has been busy making matches.'"

from Genesis Rabbah 68:4

Humorous stories about our adventures
in planning the wedding

Humorous stories from the wedding

Place wedding
photo here

בסימנא
טבא

The Blessing of Covenant

Becoming Husband and Wife

"It was the custom when a boy was born to plant a cedar tree; and when a girl was born, a pine. When they married, the trees were cut down and the wedding canopy was made from their branches."

Babylonian Talmud Gittin　*57a*

שימני כחותם על לבך
כחותם על זרועך

"We praise You, Adonai...who causes bride and groom to rejoice."
from the Sheva Berachot

Special words spoken

Memories and reflections

Blessings

What friends said

A pressed flower from the day

Place photo from the
wedding dinner here

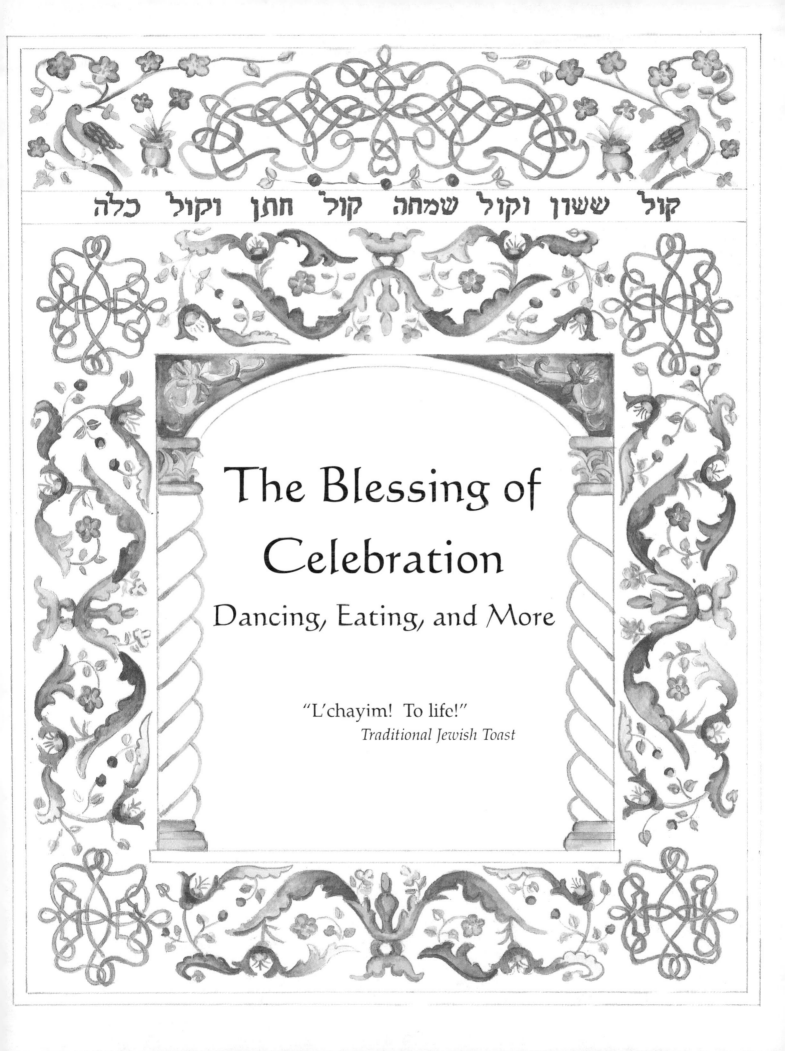

קול ששון וקול שמחה קול חתן וקול כלה

The Blessing of Celebration

Dancing, Eating, and More

"L'chayim! To life!"
Traditional Jewish Toast

The Wedding Dinner

Place photo of bride and
groom celebrating with
friends and family here

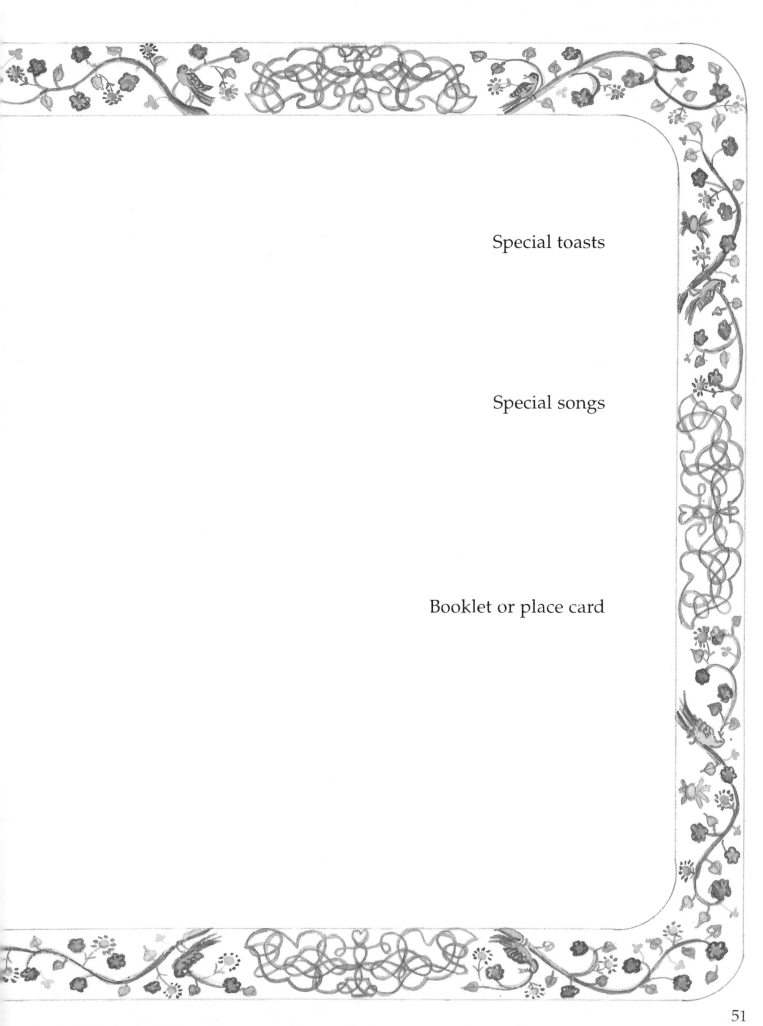

Special toasts

Special songs

Booklet or place card

Gift Record

Name	Gift	Date Acknowledged

Name   Gift   Date Acknowledged

_____

_____

_____

_____

_____

_____

_____

_____

_____

_____

_____

_____

_____

_____

_____

_____

_____

_____

_____

_____

_____

_____

_____

Gift Record

Name	Gift	Date Acknowledged

Name	Gift	Date Acknowledged

The Celebration Continues

Place honeymoon
photo here

Record of additional dinners given by friends
(traditionally called *Sheva Berachot*) and
memories of a honeymoon alone together

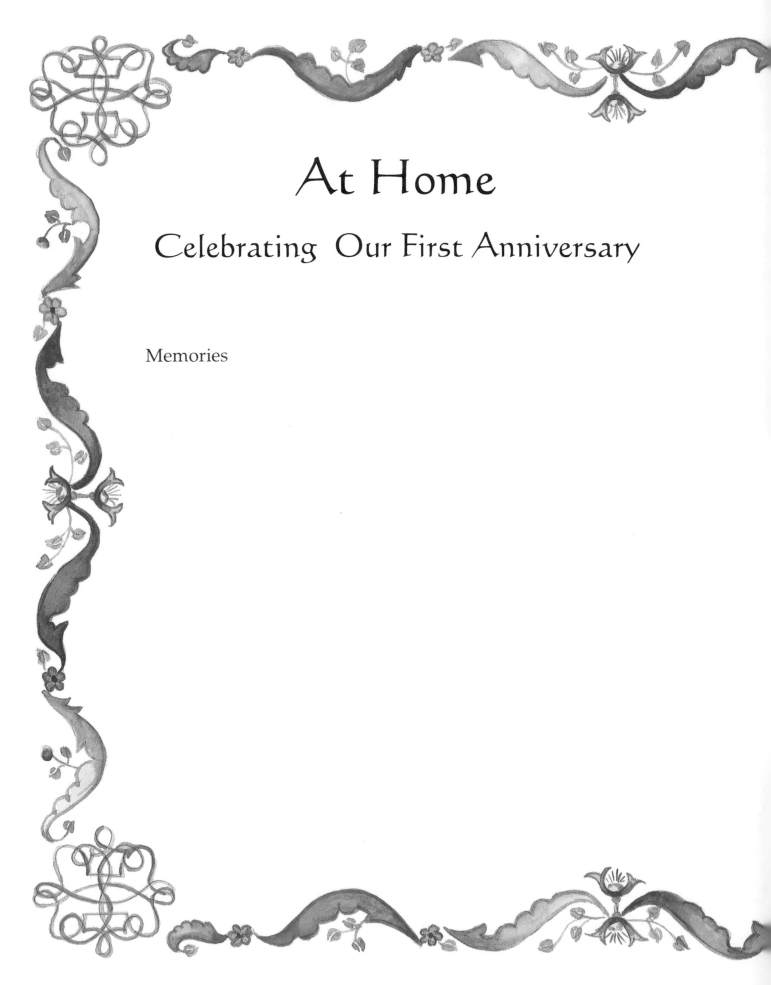

At Home

Celebrating Our First Anniversary

Memories

Baruch Atah, Adonai Eloheinu, Melech haolam, shehecheyanu vekiyemanu vehigianu lazman hazeh.

Place first anniversary
photo here

"Blessed are You, our Sovereign God, who gives us life, who sustains us, and who has caused us to reach this day."

About the Illustrations

Decorated *ketubot* are a centuries-old tradition in Jewish communities throughout the world. The *ketubah* artists found inspiration for their designs in biblical texts, wedding rituals, and Hebrew poetry. Their illustrations reflected the architecture, decorative arts, books, and gardens (i.e., the aesthetic environment) in which they were created. Thus a *ketubah* illuminated in Florence "looks" Italian, whereas one painted in Ishfahan "looks" Islamic. The illustrations in this book were inspired by these antique *ketubot*. Photographs of the originals appear in *Ketubbah* by Shalom Sabar (Philadelphia: The Jewish Publication Society, 1990).

The design for the cover and the title and presentation pages is derived from a *ketubah* painted in Acqui, Italy, in 1775. The Hebrew on the cover begins with *besiman tov* ,"with a good sign," and *mazal tov*. The Aramaic version *besimana tava* was frequently used as a preamble for Sephardic *ketubot*. The rest of the text on the cover and the text on the title page is translated: "The sounds of joy and of happiness, the voice of the groom and the voice of the bride" (Jeremiah 33:11 and the *Sheva Berachot).*

The design for the Contents page comes from eighteenth-century Holland. The original design, an engraving, resembles the wonderful floral bouquets created by the Dutch still-life masters (note the tulips). This border was the most popular decorative motif in the Sephardic communities of northern Europe. It can be found in both painted and engraved versions. The Hebrew here is *besiman tov.*

Sharing Our Lives: The inspiration for this section is a *ketubah* created in Rome in 1758. The Hebrew inscription, translated as: "I am my beloved's, and my beloved is mine," replaces the family crest, a decoration then in common usage.

Community: A *ketubah* created in Ishfahan in 1869 was the inspiration for these pages. Elements of particular note are the lion with a rising sun motif and the"Islamic" arches, the former being the Persian national symbol. The inscription here translates: "With a good sign, let me be a seal upon your heart, like the seal upon your arm. Great waters cannot extinguish love, nor can rivers overwash it" (Song of Songs 8:6,7).

A Home Together: The *ketubah* used for this section was created in Dubrovnik in 1762 and was influenced by Italian artists from the other side of the Adriatic Sea. The Hebrew here translates: "When I found the one whom my soul loves"(Song of Songs 3:4).

Tradition: The illustrations for these pages derive from a *ketubah* created in Ancona, Italy, in 1753. The Hebrew translates: "To good fortune" and "I shall betroth you to me forever" (Hosea 2:21). In the tradition of using environmentally familiar birds and flowers, those used in this book are American varieties.

Laughter: This *ketubah* is based on one created in New York in 1819. The Hebrew translates: "To good fortune, like a green garden may it come up and sprout, for the bridegroom and for the bride." The influence here is folk art found throughout the United States.

Covenant: The original *ketubah* that inspired this illustration was painted in Ferrara in 1775 and was itself inspired by Italian baroque and rococo architecture. The original design included figures of Moses, Aaron, and Samuel, as it was not uncommon to portray biblical characters. Often, the biblical namesakes of the bridegroom, his father, and sometimes the bride and her father were used. The inscription translates: " With a good sign, let me be a seal upon your heart, like the seal upon your arm" (Song of Songs 8:6).

Celebration: The design used here comes from a *ketubah* created in Corfu, dated 1714. The border pattern employed was very popular in Italy at that time, and variations can be found in many communities. The Hebrew is from the *Sheva Berachot*: "The sounds of joy and of happiness, the voice of the groom and the voice of the bride."

Marlene Lobell Ruthen